EXCAVATING THE PAST

MESOPOTAMIA

Jane Shuter

Heinemann Library
Chicago, Illinois

Photo research by Maria Joannou and
Catherine Bevan
Designed by Richard Parker and Tinstar Design
Ltd (www.tinstar.co.uk)
Printed in China by WKT Company Limited

10 09 08 07 06
10 9 8 7 6 5 4 3 2 1

**Library of Congress Cataloging-in-
Publication Data**

Shuter, Jane.
  Mesopotamia / Jane Shuter.
      p. cm. -- (Excavating the past)
  Includes bibliographical references and
index.
  ISBN 1-4034-5998-3 (lib. bdg.)
  1. Sumerians--Juvenile literature. I. Title.
II. Series.
  DS72.S558 2006
  935'.01--dc22

2005009177

Acknowledgments
The publishers would like to thank the following
for permission to reproduce photographs: British
Museum pp. **6, 9, 11, 20, 21, 22, 27, 32, 34, 35,
36, 37, 39** both, **41**; Corbis pp. **14** (Bettmann), **26**
(Gianni Dagli Orti), **30** (Barney Burstein), **38** (Nik
Wheeler), **39** top (Nik Wheeler); Getty Images pp.
42 (Mario Tama), **8** (Hulton Archive); Hilprecht
Collection, Friedrich-Schiller University, Jena p. **19**;
Michael Holford p. **16**; Photo Scala, Florence pp.
10, 13, 15, 23, 28, 29; Scala p. **43**; Taisei
Corporation, Tokyo p. **24** (NHK); University of
Pennsylvania Museum of Archaeology &
Anthropolgy pp. **7, 25, 33**; Werner Forman
Archive pp. **12, 17**.

Cover photograph of the ziggurat at Ur
reproduced with permission of Robert Harding
Picture Library (Richard Ashworth). Small picture
of a gold figure reproduced with permission of Art
Archive (Musée du Louvre Paris / Dagli Orti.)

Illustrations by Jeff Edwards and Eikon Illustration

The publishers would like to thank Jonathan
Tenney of the Oriental Institute at the University of
Chicago for his assistance in the preparation of this
book.

Every effort has been made to contact
copyright holders of any material reproduced in
this book. Any omissions will be rectified in
subsequent printings if notice is given to the
publishers.

CONTENTS

Dates B.C.E. **and** C.E.

B.C.E. after a date means "before the common era." The years count down to 0.

C.E. before a date stands for "of the common era." It means that the year is counted from after the year 0.

Archaeology and Mesopotamia 4
  Rediscovering the Sumerians 6

The Importance of Writing 8

City-states 14
  What was a city like?...18
  Outside the city 20

Beliefs and Burials..22
  Temples 24
  Burial and the afterlife..26
  Royal tombs 27

Daily Life...28

Skilled Work 34

Travel and Trade 38

Archaeology in Modern Iraq 42

Timeline 44
Timeline of Archaeology..45
Glossary 46
Further Reading 47
Index...48

ARCHAEOLOGY AND MESOPOTAMIA

Several different civilizations controlled parts of ancient Mesopotamia at different times. We are going to look at the first of these people: the Sumerians. The Sumerian people lived in southern Mesopotamia, now part of Iraq, between about 3750 B.C.E. and 2004 B.C.E. They lived by and between the Tigris and Euphrates Rivers, in land that was low and flat, with few trees. This part of the world is very hot and dry.

The two rivers

The Sumerians lived close to the Tigris and Euphrates Rivers to get water to grow crops, wash and cook. They were very different rivers. The Euphrates was a slow, winding river that flooded each spring. When the water went down it left banks of thick, rich mud that made an excellent soil to grow crops in. However the Euphrates often flooded badly, affecting villages and towns. Either river could change its course as the sea level gradually rose. The Tigris was not as slow as the Euphrates and did not often flood. However, this meant almost all the water for growing crops had to be hauled from the river by hand.

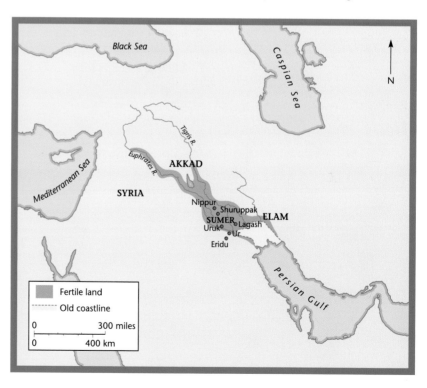

▷ The Sumerians settled the fertile land around the Tigris and Euphrates Rivers. This map shows how much further inland the ancient coastline was.

Black Sea

Caspian Sea

N

Tigris R.

Euphrates R.

AKKAD

Mediterranean Sea

SYRIA

Nippur
Shuruppak
SUMER   Lagash   ELAM
Uruk   Ur
Eridu

Persian Gulf

■ Fertile land
---- Old coastline

0   300 miles
0   400 km

WHO IS Juris Zarins?

Juris Zarins was born in Germany in 1945, but his family moved to the United States soon after he was born. He studied anthropology at the Universities of Nebraska and Chicago before going on to work at Southwest Missouri State University. Zarins was the person who first used satellite photos to work out where the ancient Sumerian coastline was.

Problems for archaeologists

Mesopotamia had few trees and no rocks, so people used mud bricks and reeds for their buildings. Mud bricks wear out and need constant repair, or even rebuilding. New towns and cities were built on top of old ones, and ancient sites can be spotted because they stand above ground level, making a platform called a "tell." Although tells make ancient cities easier to spot, most of the ancient buildings have crumbled away so there are fewer remains for archaeologists to study.

Water is power

In ancient times different groups of people lived all over Mesopotamia. They often lived peacefully with each other. But they sometimes fought each other, too. Because rivers were so important to life in Mesopotamia, the people who lived there struggled to control the water. In times where the line of the rivers changed or they began to run dry, people could run out of water. Some archaeologists think that the Sumerians became more important, and began to control larger areas of land, because the Euphrates River shifted toward them, in about 3000 B.C.E. They believe satellite photos of the area show the old coastline, and where the Tigris and Euphrates Rivers once ran.

Living on the edge

In 2002, Saddam Hussein, then ruler of Iraq, drained the marshes between the Tigris and Euphrates Rivers. Before he did this, Marsh Arabs still lived in the area, building homes and boats very similar to those shown on seals from Sumerian times. People studied the way the Marsh Arabs lived to help them understand how the Sumerians lived.

Rediscovering the Sumerians

After they were taken over by the Elamites (in about 2004 B.C.E.) the Sumerians were forgotten. It was not until the 1870s that archaeologists rediscovered them. Mesopotamia was in an area many Europeans and Americans called "the Bible Lands." So when they went looking for archaeological sites in Mesopotamia, they were looking for people mentioned in the Christian Bible.

A new people

Long before the 1860s, archaeologists had found writing tablets made out of pieces of clay. People had written on these tablets by pressing a sliced reed into the clay, making a wedge shape. Archaeologists called this writing cuneiform. When the tablets were dated, cuneiform was found to be one of the earliest scripts. Archaeologists first thought the earliest cuneiform tablets were written by the Akkadian people, who lived in northern Mesopotamia from about 2400 B.C.E. Then they found some Akkadian writings that seemed to be dictionaries. They gave lists of Akkadian words next to lists of words in an unknown language, possibly one earlier than Akkadian.

Fantasy or Fact?

Once the Sumerians were rediscovered, some archaeologists began to insist they were different from all other Mesopotamian people. In 1906 Eduard Meyer insisted their baldness, size, the roundness of their heads, and their clothes meant they must have come to Mesopotamia from far away. He based this on a study of some skeletons, but mostly on pictures of people on artifacts, which showed styles of hair and clothing. Modern historians believe that these differences have been exaggerated.

Pottery pieces

Archaeologists study the designs and shapes of pots very carefully. If one shape or design is used by several groups in one area and nowhere else, it is likely that these groups all shared the same culture.

Out of the shadows

In 1877 Ernest de Sarzec, a Frenchman working in Basra, became interested in the archaeology of the area. He explored the ancient tells near the town and decided to dig into the one the local people called Telloh. He found the remains of large temples and other buildings made from mud brick. It was clearly an early city.

He also found statues of a ruler, probably the ruler of the city, called Gudea. Finally he found some clay tablets with writing on. The writing matched the unknown language found in the Akkadian dictionaries. He took everything he had found so far back to France and sold it to the Louvre Museum, which then paid for him to keep excavating. He had found the first evidence of where the Sumerians had lived.

Archaeology Challenge

Archaeologists have to try to work out how people in the past lived by looking at the things they have left behind. Comparing these things helps archaeologists understand societies better. Social archaeologists have made lists to compare societies, so that archaeologists do not all use different systems, which would be confusing. For instance, these lists say that early civilizations must have cities with temples and public buildings, a strong government, people doing different jobs (from rulers to farmers), writing, studying of maths and the stars, and trade with other people. All early civilizations, including those in China, Egypt, Sumer, and the Indus Valley, fit this list.

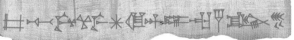

△ *Archaeologists have been trying to uncover the secrets of Mesopotamia for many decades.*

THE IMPORTANCE OF WRITING

Sumerian is not like any other language there has ever been. Archaeologists were lucky that people carried on writing and speaking Sumerian for hundreds of years after the Sumerians were taken over—in the way that Latin is still taught today. The Akkadians made dictionary tablets of Sumerian. So, to be able to read Sumerian, people had to be able to read Akkadian.

The Behistan Rock

The Behistan Rock is part of a 1,700 foot (518 meter) high cliff in northern Mesopotamia. In about 520 B.C.E. a Persian king had descriptions of his victories carved onto it, in Persian and two other languages. In 1835 Englishman Henry Rawlinson decided to find out what the other languages were. He climbed the cliff and began to copy the writing, using ladders and ropes to hang with his hands free. It was slow, dangerous work and he was concerned his copying might not be accurate. So he hired a local boy to go up and down the cliff face, pushing soft papier-mâché bricks onto the wall to get prints of the writing.

A better way

Rawlinson used papier-mâché to copy the shapes of the cuneiform writing. But papier-mâché takes a while to make and has to have just the right amount of water. It would not have damaged rock-carved letters, but might damage pottery ones. Modern archaeologists take copies with latex, a rubbery mixture that can be sprayed or smoothed on and peels off easily.

WHO WAS Henry Rawlinson?

Henry Creswicke Rawlinson was born in 1810 and joined the East India Company in 1827 to train as a soldier. He was good at learning languages. He went to Persia in 1833 to help reorganize the Persian army and stayed. He worked on the Behistan Rock and led one excavation, at Borsippa in northern Mesopotamia. He died in 1895.

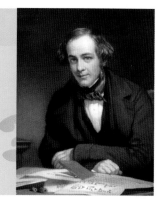

Meaning	Pictogram (ca. 3500–3000 B.C.E.)	Early Cuneiform (ca. 2400–1800 B.C.E.)	Later Cuneiform (ca. 700 B.C.E.)
Water, stream			
Mountain			
Plough			
Grain			
Pig			

▷ *This table shows some of the picture symbols used as a form of writing in Mesopotamia.*

Cracking the code

Back in England Rawlinson worked on translating the Old Persian writings from the Behistan Rock. This alone took years. Then he began on the unknown cuneiform writing. By this time other language scholars were interested in it, too. These included Jules Oppert, a Frenchman, Edward Hincks, an Irish clergyman, and Isidor Lowenstern from Sweden. By 1850 they had most of the languages worked out. It was at about this time that the dictionary tablets were found at Nineveh, in the far north of Mesopotamia.

Moving on to Sumerian

Until the early 1900s, language scholars worked at copying the many Sumerian tablets that had been discovered by archaeologists. They really needed many different examples of Sumerian before they could begin translating. This was made more complicated because Sumerian itself changed. It moved from simple pictures in the earliest tablets and seals, to a combination of pictures and sounds, to a written language using sounds only. By the 1920s and 1930s, much of the work was done, and we can now read many hundreds of different Sumerian writings.

◁ *It has taken language scholars many years to work out what the pictures on seals like this mean, but they have eventually discovered a lot about Sumerian life.*

Who did the writing?

There are thousands of Sumerian clay tablets. Some even had clay envelopes, to keep the document inside safe. But not all Sumerians could read or write. The Sumerian written language was very complicated. It took years to learn. Some important people had the time and took the trouble to learn to write, but most writing was done by scribes. Most of the evidence we have about scribes comes from the clay tablets unearthed by archaeologists.

◁ *This stone statue, left as an offering to the gods, may show a scribe.*

Archaeology Challenge

A cuneiform scholar first had to work out what the different symbols meant. The next problem was which way to read Sumerian—from left to right and down from the top as we read, or not? Scribes wrote left to right and top to bottom on the first side. Then they turned the page by lifting the bottom end up and flipping the tablet over, so the bottom became the top on the other side. They then wrote on the second side right to left, working up from the bottom.

Scribes

A scribe was called a *dubsar* in Sumerian. Almost all scribes were men. They were mostly the sons of important people, because only people who could read and write could do the most important job of running the country. Also ordinary Sumerians could not afford to pay teachers' fees. Students were taught daily in a school called "the tablet house." Archaeologists have not yet found one of these. Several temples had their own tablet schools that trained scribes especially to be priests.

A typical school day

Students had six days off a month. Otherwise, they went to school every day, from sunrise to sunset. They took their lunch with them.

What did they learn?

The first thing students learned was how to make clay tablets and split reeds to make their "pens." Next, they learned how to use the pens. They moved on to learning hundreds of symbols. Most of them stood for different words in the Sumerian language. They learned by copying the same piece of writing over and over again. They probably recited it as they wrote. Writing was the most important skill that scribes learned. However, they learned math, too. They needed to be good at math to work as a government or temple official. One of the tablets archaeologists have found many copies of talks about students being beaten for being late, lazy, or playing truant.

How long did it take?

It took many years to learn to be a scribe. Those who stayed the longest learned more—astronomy, medicine, music, and engineering, for example. Some never left the tablet house. They became teachers, or made a living by copying famous stories, poems, and other things that people wanted copied.

▷ *This tablet has one of the passages students copied on it.*

Lists and letters

What do all the ancient Sumerian writings found by archaeologists tells us? The earliest kinds of Sumerian writing, the pictures, were used mainly for very simple things. So people kept count of the number of sheep they had, or had sold, by using a number and a sheep picture. A person showed he owned something by putting his special seal on it.

EYEWITNESS

"Keep an eye on the man who plants the barley seed. Make sure he drops the seeds evenly, about two fingers deep in the soil."

From the Sumerian tablet that is the first farming instruction book.

As the language got more complicated people began to make lists, write down laws, recipes, and medical prescriptions, and keep records of how the stars moved. By the end of the Sumerian period people were writing stories, love poems, letters, proverbs, and even lamentations—writings about how the Sumerian cities were not as great as they had once been.

A modern outlook?

Here are a few Sumerian sayings with a modern feel:
- "Don't stand there with your mouth open—you'll swallow a fly!"
- "Catch your fox first, before you make a collar from it."
- "My wife is at the shrine, my mother by the river, and I am at home, starving to death!"
- "He who has silver may be happy, he who has barley may be glad, but he who has nothing can sleep at night, without fear of loss."

▷ *Many tablets were used by scribes to keep lists of wages, stores of food, and numbers of workers, so that the city could be run efficiently. This tablet is a list of the number of farmers growing crops around the city, and the amount of land each has been given in payment for their work for the king.*

The story of the flood

The first ever story about a great flood is Sumerian. Archaeologists did not find the complete story, but enough to work out the rest. The story was written in about 2900 B.C.E., and the ruler mentioned in the story, Ziusudra, ruled Shuruppak, a city by the Euphrates River. Archaeologists have found evidence to show that the area around Shuruppak was flooded at about that time.

In this story, the gods of Sumer become angry with the Sumerians. Most of the gods wanted to destroy the Sumerians, but the god Enki warned one good man, King Ziusudra, that the other gods were going to send a flood to wipe out all men.

▽ Other Mesopotamian peoples, the Akkadians and the Babylonians, told a similar story, with different details. This Akkadian seal shows scenes from the story.

So Ziusudra built a huge boat for himself and his family. The storm came and lasted seven days and seven nights. The whole of southern Mesopotamia was flooded and everyone was killed except for Ziusudra and his family in their large boat.

CITY-STATES

The earliest Sumerian people lived in small settlements of related families along the Tigris and Euphrates Rivers. Some historians think the most important men in the group ran things, choosing one man to rule if there was an emergency, such as war.

The earliest Sumerian city that archaeologists have found so far is Eridu, first excavated in 1946 by Fuad Safar and Seton Lloyd, Iraqi and American archaeologists working for the Iraq Antiquities Directorate. Eridu was a small settlement as early as 5500 B.C.E., and grew into a city. The city then grew to become a city-state. The same happened in Uruk, another city built on a settlement lived in before Sumerian times.

By 3000 B.C.E. the Sumerians were living in several separate city-states. These were made up of a large, walled, city and the lands around it. City-states had one ruler, who was both the king and the most important priest. The Sumerians believed in many different gods and goddesses, but each city-state had one god or goddess that they believed looked after them with special care.

△ *Stratigraphy is when archaeologists excavate a site layer by layer, carefully recording what was found in each layer. Cities often have many different layers, so archaeologists find older and older evidence of the city as they go deeper.*

WHO WAS Gilgamesh?

Gilgamesh is one of the heroes of many Sumerian stories. He is said to have been the king of Uruk. He is the 38th king on a long list of kings called the Sumerian King List. Where historians can check the list, it seems to be quite accurate. The stories about Gilgamesh are not about how he ruled Uruk, but about his many travels and adventures while looking for the secret of eternal life.

How were city-states organized?

The most important person in a city-state was the ruler. He made all the decisions from the taxes people must pay, to when to go to war. The king was also the most important priest, and was seen as the link between the gods and goddesses of Sumer and ordinary people.

Different officials ran Sumer for the king. Many of them were all scribes. Some of them traveled all over the city-state, making sure that taxes were paid and people were fed, even in the poorest farming areas.

Next came the craft workers who made pottery, furniture and jewelry, as well as things from gold, silver, and bronze. Archaeologists have found the remains of their workshops, and the artifacts they made, while excavating Sumerian cities. There were many less important workers who still had special skills—butchers and bakers, for example. Almost all these workers were men. Women were expected to look after the house and children.

△ *This copper head of a king is thought to be Sargon, who ruled Sumer and Akkad from 2350 to 2279 B.C.E.*

War

Once the Sumerians began to organize themselves into city-states, they began to go to war more often. They fought each other, mostly over land and water. Sometimes several small city-states joined together to fight one big one. If they were threatened by other peoples, city-states joined together to fight the outsiders.

Organization

In many early civilizations, every man trained to fight when the ruler needed them. Sumerian city-states may have had full-time armies. These armies would have been important in the Sumerians' rise to power—making them stronger than other Mesopotamian peoples. However, Sumerians fought among themselves so much that they weakened each other and were taken over. When the city went to war the king led the army.

A picture of war

The Standard of Ur, which was found in the tomb of a Sumerian king, shows an army coming back from war. There are lines of chariots pulled by donkeys, and soldiers in armor carrying heavy maces. It also shows prisoners, stripped of their clothes and bleeding, being hauled in front of the king. We still do not know what the standard was used for.

Weapons and armor

Sumerian soldiers fought mainly on foot. They used spears with metal blades, axes, clubs, bows and arrows, and daggers. Chariots were used to transport the armor and weapons to battle and were also used in fighting. One soldier drove the chariot, while another rode behind him and threw spears. Chariots were heavy and slow, so were probably used to break up the enemy soldiers, while the foot soldiers followed close behind to fight.

Early Sumerian armor was made from leather, sometimes with metal discs on it. The foot soldiers on the Standard of Ur wear leather helmets and leather capes with metal discs. The discs gave the soldier some protection from weapons, but were not as heavy as armor made entirely from metal. The archers and charioteers did not wear capes, as they needed their arms free to fight. Archaeologists have found several copper helmets from later Sumerian times.

△ *This is the heavy marble end of a Sumerian club. Soldiers had to get close to the enemy to use it, unlike using a spear, but it was deadly.*

Tactics

Because they had the first full-time armies, the Sumerians are the first people we know worked out battle tactics, such as fighting in a group, all marching in step. As well as battles, the Sumerians also besieged cities, cutting the city off from the outside world and attacking it over and over again. So as well as soldiers, the army had engineers who built ladders, and perhaps towers, to get up the city walls. They also had soldiers who were trained to tunnel through city walls.

> ### EYEWITNESS
> "Inside, outside, is the same: only death. Outside, the enemy's spear. Inside, starvation's knife."
>
> *Part of a Sumerian lamentation, describing a siege.*

What was a city like?

Sumerian cities were not all the same shape and size, but all of those excavated by archaeologists have had some of the same things:

- a tell: a build up of refuse
- a wall around the outside
- a ziggurat temple, palace, and important government buildings in the center of the city
- at least one public square
- large areas for storing food
- workshops and homes on the edges of the city. Each area had its own communal ovens, shrines, and water ditches.
- wide streets
- lots of smaller, twisty streets off the main streets.

▽ *This is a modern artist's idea of what the city of Ur may have looked like, according to archaeological evidence.*

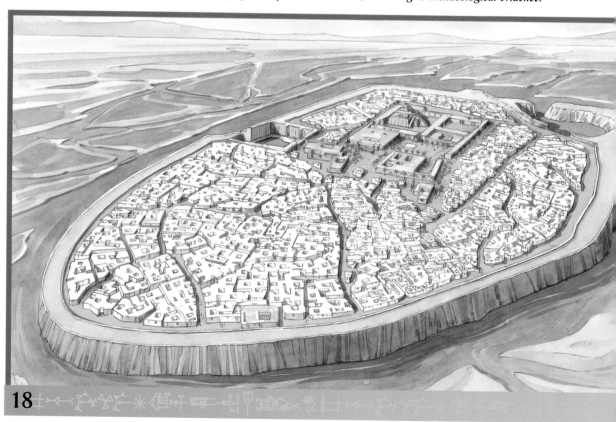

The city wall kept the city safe, but also stopped it growing. Archaeologists think people probably built upwards when there was no more space to build at ground level. As the buildings have crumbled to ground level, there is no evidence to prove this. Archaeologists have also found buildings outside the city walls of some cities, usually small homes and workshops. They think that maybe the least important people in the city were sometimes forced to live outside the walls when the city got too crowded.

Who lived in cities?

Not all Sumerians lived in cities, but many of the most important people did. The ruler and his most important officials lived there, as did the many priests and priestesses who worked in the temples. Craft workers and their families lived in the cities. Archaeologists have found workshops and the tools and equipment of jewelers, potters, leather workers, metalworkers, carpenters, and basket makers. Then there were the people who provided food and drink: the butchers, bakers, and brewers. Archaeologists have also found the remains of bars and restaurants.

Archaeology Challenge

Thermoluminescence is a way of dating baked clay—pottery, bricks, or tablets. A small sample of the clay is heated to 842°F (450°C), at which point it gives off a burst of light. The longer the burst of light, the older the baked clay is. Careful measurement and comparison of the lengths of the bursts of light help archaeologists work out accurate dates.

△ This is a clay tablet plan of the city of Nippur, made in about 1500 B.C.E. It is the earliest known plan of a city, and matches very well what archaeologists have found at Nippur.

Outside the city

A city-state could not have survived without the many people who lived and worked in small settlements outside the city—the farmers. Each city-state had to grow enough food to feed its people and, hopefully, to store some food for times when there were problems such as a bad harvest or flooding. Unlike the Nile River, which rose slowly between late July and September every year, the Tigris and the Euphrates Rivers rose at any time between April and early June. When they did they could flood with hardly any warning, especially the Tigris.

△ *One side of the Standard of Ur shows Sumerian soldiers at war. The other side shows peacetime life, with farmers herding cattle, sheep, and goats, and fishermen with their catch.*

To control the flooding as much as possible, the Sumerians built up the side of the rivers, in levees (steps), using bricks or reed mats to stop the levees being washed away. They then dug a complicated system of canals with smaller trenches running off them, to carry water from the rivers to the farmland. These canals were important in helping to make flooding less of a problem, as they could carry off some of the floodwater and store it. The canals were fitted with boards that could be closed to keep the water in and lifted to get it out. The canals and trenches had to be cleared regularly, so that they did not clog up with mud.

Archaeology Challenge

Aerial photography helps archaeologists to work out where irrigation canals once ran in Mesopotamia. Photographs taken when the Sun is quite low and shadows are long can show up canal patterns that are not clear when archaeologists are at ground level.

The farming year

Farmers plowed the soil in the fall and then sowed the seeds. They used simple wooden tools, including plows pulled by cattle or donkeys. The most important crop was grain, mostly barley. This was used to make bread and beer, the basic Sumerian food and drink. Archaeologists have found drawings on clay tablets of a machine for sowing seeds deeply and evenly.

EYEWITNESS

"Do not let the barley grow so tall that it bends over itself before you harvest it. Cut it when it is at its tallest."

From the Sumerian tablet that is the first farming instruction book.

As well as grain, farmers grew vegetables and fruit. Archaeologists have found a poem that shows that farmers grew crops that needed special care, such as lettuce, in the shade of their fruit trees.

The Sumerians kept sheep, goats, and cattle for meat and milk. There is evidence that they hunted wild animals, too.

Archaeology Challenge

Soil analysis can tell archaeologists a lot about the crops farmers may have grown. Archaeologists have found more barley than wheat in their excavations. Soil analysis shows that the soil was better for growing barley than wheat, because of the levels of salt and other minerals in it. They would have preferred the crop that grew best. So it supports the archaeologists findings that the Sumerians grew more barley than wheat.

▽ *This carving shows farmers milking cows and making butter in large pottery jars.*

BELIEFS AND BURIALS

The Sumerians believed in many different gods and goddesses that controlled every aspect of Sumerian life, including natural disasters, such as flooding. Most gods and goddesses controlled more than one part of life. So Enki was god of the sea and water, but also god of knowledge and wisdom. It was important to keeps gods and goddesses happy by providing them with the same things as people needed: a home, food, and affection. The home had to be the biggest and best home in the city, which is why the ziggurat temples reached so high. The food had to be the best of the food, and affection was shown by constant prayers and offerings.

The three most important gods were An, the sky god; Enlil, god of the air; and Enki, the water god. The most important goddess, Inanna, controlled both love and war. Although the gods lived forever, they acted just like humans. They could be happy, sad, jealous, and kind. They often bickered among themselves, like a large family.

▷ *This impression from a seal, found by archaeologists in Uruk, shows a Sumerian ruler feeding his people (shown as animals). The tall, curving bundles of reeds are the goddess Inanna, goddess of the city of Uruk.*

Gods of the city-states

Each Sumerian city-state had one god or goddess who they thought looked after their city-state with special care. For example, Enki, the water god, was the special god of Eridu. Most cities had several temples, but the biggest, more central, temple belonged to the god of the city. The most important priest, and the link between the people and the gods, was the ruler of the city. He was expected to keep temples in good repair and build new ones. The bigger and more beautifully decorated the temples were, the happier the gods and goddesses would be.

Where did people worship?

Archaeologists have found that there was an open space in front of each temple, probably for people to gather in for religious festivals. Many of these festivals were tied into the farming year to ask for a good crop at planting time. However, people mostly worshipped at chapels built on street corners in the cities or, if they lived in the countryside, at shrines set up in villages or by the roadside. They also had small shrines in their own homes. Chapels and shrines would have a statue of the god or goddess with space to leave offerings. Each person had one god or goddess as their special protector. They prayed to this god or goddess about personal matters.

Constant prayer

The Sumerians could not spend all their time praying to their gods and goddesses, so they left these statues (below) at temples to pray for them. They are called votive statues. The statues often had big, adoring eyes. Sometimes these statues were left when a person wanted a special favor from the gods. Most were left just to show the gods that the person who had left the statue worshipped the gods.

EYEWITNESS

"Gazing up at us out of the shadows were two pairs of appalling eyes. Huge black eyes with gleaming white eyeballs. They were set in the faces of a bearded man and a woman each holding a cup."

Part of a description by the archaeologist Mary Chubb of the discovery of votive statues at the temple at Eshnunna in 1932.

Temples

The earliest Mesopotamian temples that archaeologists have found were large rectangular mud-brick buildings. However, because temples had to be kept in good repair, they were often built over, or around, and so grew in size over time. Archaeologists found that the temple at Eridu, an early city, had twelve temples built one over another.

By 2000 B.C.E. people were building ziggurats—temples with three levels, one on top of the other, each smaller than the last. At the very top was the shrine where the statue of the god or goddess of the temple was kept and cared for. Archaeologists have so far only found one ziggurat in each city they have excavated, although they have found other smaller temples. They think that this means that the ziggurat was built for the god or goddess that took special care of the city. Ziggurats had a walled courtyard in front of them and various buildings all around the walls inside the courtyard. Most temples also owned some farmland outside the city. The ziggurat to the god or goddess of the city owned a lot of land and animals.

Virtual reality

Modern computer techniques used with archaeological evidence can help archaeologists reconstruct what towns or temples looked like when they were newly built and decorated. This is a virtual reality computer image of the ziggurat at Ur, which was carefully set out so that its four corners point north, south, east, and west. There was only one way into a ziggurat, by steep steps that went up the side that ran from north to east. Archaeologists have found evidence that the walls of at least some ziggurats were painted in black, white, red, and blue.

The temples were run by priests and priestesses, who looked after a statue of the god or goddess of the temple with great care. This included running the religious ceremonies that happened every day and on special holy days. There were also priests and priestesses who did not take part in the care of the god, or in the various religious ceremonies. Instead, they took care of business —running all the temple lands, making sure the crops were planted and harvested and the workers paid.

The clay tablets discovered by archaeologists tell us that the work of all priests and priestesses was carefully divided up and sorted into different levels of importance. Priests and priestesses had to come from good families and be fit and healthy. They came to temple schools to learn their job, which included learning to read and write. The most important priest was the ruler of the city. The least important priests were the scribes who kept the day-to-day records. Temples also had many servants to provide food, drink, and clothes for the priests and for the god. The tablets tell us that two meals a day were brought and left near the altar for the god of the temple to "eat." It is not clear what actually happened to the food—archaeologists assume that the priests ate it.

△ *King Sargon, who was an Akkadian but ruled Sumer and Akkad, made his daughter high priestess of the temple to Nanna in Ur. He did this to try to get more acceptance for his family among Sumerians.*

Burial and the afterlife

The Sumerians believed in an afterlife where the dead person needed to take possessions from this life with them. At one of the earliest Sumerian cemeteries, at Eridu, about 1,000 graves of ordinary people were found. They were buried in a simple hole in the ground, sometimes wrapped in reed matting and with some food and pottery. Some dogs were buried with their owners, a meatbone in the mouths for their journey to the afterlife.

EYEWITNESS

"Our aim was to understand the history, not to fill museums with curious objects. The more rich the cemetery looked like being, the more important it was to leave it alone until we had provided a time frame for it from the rest of the site."

Leonard Woolley, explaining why his team did not immediately excavate the cemetery at Ur as soon as they realized it was there, in 1922.

△ *This dagger was dropped by robbers looting a "royal" tomb, and lay there until Woolley and his team excavated it. It is made of gold, with a* lapis lazuli *handle.*

The cemetery at Ur

The most famous Sumerian cemetery is at Ur, excavated by Leonard Woolley in the 1920s. The archaeologists found over 2,000 graves in 2 separate cemeteries. Many were the graves of ordinary people, but about sixteen were clearly the tombs of important people, now called "royal" tombs. They were big tombs, once filled with beautiful and expensive possessions. The people in them had been buried with possessions and also with servants, real people who were killed so they could travel with the tomb owner to the afterlife. The first "royal" tombs Woolley excavated had been robbed. The robbers had left behind a single golden dagger, which showed how beautiful the things they had stolen must have been. Then, between 1927 and 1928 they found tombs that still had some of their treasure.

Playing games

This board game was found in the tomb of the man buried below Pu-abi, possibly her husband, and king of Ur. The game was a race game for two players. The different patterns had different meanings and could be lucky or unlucky.

Royal tombs

As archaeologists worked toward the royal tombs they found the bodies of 63 well-dressed men and women. Each had a cup that had probably held poison. With them were several oxen wearing silver collars. Archaeologists think they were being sent to keep the king company in the afterlife.

WHO WAS Pu-abi?

Archaeologists know that Pu-abi was an important woman in Ur. There was about 40 feet (12.2 meters) of gold ribbon entwined in her hair, and she was buried with a large amount of beautifully made jewelry. Twenty-three women were buried with her. She was buried after her husband, because her tomb was exactly above his. It was probably the gravediggers making her tomb who found his and looted it. They put one of her boxes over the hole they had made, to hide their crime. Archaeologists have not been able to work out if Pu-abi was a queen, a priestess, or both.

DID YOU KNOW? Pu-abi had a drinking straw made of pure gold.

DAILY LIFE

Much of what we know about daily life in Sumer comes from their written records, the clay tablets. Archaeologists have not found any Sumerian money, suggesting that the Sumerians did not use it. Clay tablets show that people who worked for a temple or for the king were paid in barley, beer, bread, and wool. They were also given somewhere to live. It seems that everyone had a rough idea of what things were worth compared to a sack of barley or, if things were valuable, a lump of silver.

As far as archaeologists can tell, everyone in a city-state was expected to work for the good of the city-state, at whatever they were trained to do. The king ruled everyone, and people had to pay him taxes. As the Sumerians did not use money, these taxes were paid in two ways. First, people gave the government a part of what they produced, from food to jewelry. Second, they had to spend a certain number of days working for the government, either in the army or on building works, such as canal digging. In return, the government made sure they had shelter, food, and enough wool to make clothes.

Banquets

Banquets and feasts were important to the Sumerians. Kings held banquets to celebrate holy days and victories in war. This stone carving shows a king of Lagash taking part in a religious ceremony. In the top row the king, the biggest person, is shown with a basket of bricks on his head. This was to show how important it was for the king to build and repair cities and temples. In the bottom row, the king is at the feast held at the end of the ceremony. Ordinary people celebrated events by sharing the best meal they could make.

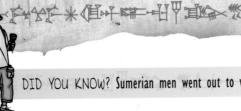

Family life

Families were very important in Sumer, and people often lived in large family groups. Parents arranged their children's marriages; some couples may not even have met until their wedding day. We know about the way marriages were arranged because the parents drew up written agreements, contracts, with each other when the arrangements were made. Without this contract a couple were not properly married. We do not know much about the actual wedding ceremony, although we do know there would have been a feast to celebrate the contracts to marry.

Archaeology Challenge

Social historians try to reconstruct how people lived in the past by using the evidence uncovered by archaeologists. So they know that family life was important, that marriages were made by contract, and that the eldest son of a family inherited everything when his father died. There is written evidence for all of this. However there is not definite evidence that boys learned their fathers' trades. There are some hints on written tablets, and they know it happened in similar societies, such as ancient Egypt.

▽ *Many couples came to love each other, even if they hardly knew each other before they married. This statue, made in about 2700 B.C.E., was found by archaeologists at the temple of Ianna at Nippur. It shows a loving husband and wife showing their devotion to the goddess.*

What did the Sumerians look like?

Forensic archaeologists have studied the skeletons in
Sumerian burials to work out what they would have looked
like. They were short and solid, not thin. They had thin
lips and thin, straight noses. Their eyes may have sloped
downward. Archaeologists suggest that they were probably
dark haired, dark eyed, and dark skinned. There is evidence
from the tablets to confirm the hair color. The Sumerians
often refer to themselves as "the dark-haired people."

Archaeologists have not found any Sumerian clothes.
However we know from the tablets that they made their
clothes from wool. This is supported by the fact that they
kept many sheep. The images of Sumerians on carvings
and statues show that in early times Sumerian men wore
kilts from the waist to the knee, while women wore
layered skirts, with a shawl around their shoulders. Later
women wore long tunics and men wore shorter tunics.
The fabric was often looped and bunched. Working
people always wore simple clothes that were easy to
move and work in.

Fantasy or Fact?

The first people to describe the
Sumerians thought that all the
men had shaven heads and
were clean-shaven, as many
of the statues and carvings
showed them this way. Later
discoveries showed that, in fact,
they sometimes had beards
and hair on their heads.

All dressed up

We know that rich women wore jewelry and make
up, because these things have been found in their
graves. This piece of jewelry was found in the grave
of Pu-abi, in Ur. It belonged to Pu-abi, but the
women buried with her were also wearing beautiful
jewelry, though not as grand as this.

Sumerian homes

Farmers who lived outside the cities mostly lived in one-roomed homes built from bundles of reeds. Sumerian houses in cities were made from mud bricks. The poor lived in just one room and palaces had many rooms. Archaeologists who have excavated these homes know their size and shape for certain because the outline of the ground floor still survives. They know that homes were arranged around a central courtyard and that walls were sometimes as much as 8 feet (2.4 meters) thick, to keep out the heat. They know kitchens were often part of the courtyard, with an open brick hearth against the courtyard wall. They know there were bathrooms in many homes.

Archaeologists assume homes had windows, to let in some light, but that they were small and high up, to keep the heat and rain out.

▷ *Archaeologists also assume that some homes had a second level, maybe even a third, because there are the remains of poles that may have held up a balcony, but they cannot be entirely sure.*

Keeping clean

Sumerian homes with several rooms, those of craft workers and more important people, quite often had a room that was used as a bathroom and toilet. Archaeologists have found these rooms in houses at Ur. The floor of the room is coated in waterproof bitumen and slopes towards a drain in the center. That drain leads to a bigger street drain that carries the water and waste out of the city. People washed by having water poured all over them, while washing with "soap" made from fat and ashes. It is not clear whether people used the drain as a toilet by crouching over it or, like the ancient Egyptians, they used a jar with a seat as a toilet and emptied it down the drain regularly, with extra water to carry the waste away.

Eating well

The Sumerians ate two meals a day—breakfast and a larger main meal in the early evening. It is likely that weak beer was the most usual drink, and that bread, cheese, vegetables, oil, and porridge were the most usual foods.

Fantasy or Fact?

Archaeologists first thought that the recipe tablets they found were medical writings. They thought that they told doctors how to prepare herbal medicines, in the way that some ancient Egyptian medical texts were known to do. It was not until they translated many of them and found they used meat (which herbal cures do not) that they realized they had the world's first recipe book. They later found medical writings, too.

◁ Doctors used fresh plants when they could, but they also stored dried plants in containers, like this stone box.

WHO WAS Martin Levey?

Martin Levey studied chemistry and then the history of medicine at college. In 1953 S. N. Kramer, an American who had studied the Sumerian clay tablets for years, called Levey in to help him with a tablet that Kramer thought might be medical writings. While Kramer carefully worked out as much of the text as he could, Levey worked out the technical words and processes. As they worked out more of the text, they became more confident about meanings, as they were used over again and seemed to fit. Levey went on to study other ancient medical texts.

Keeping healthy

The Sumerians had two kinds of doctors to call on if they were sick. The *asu* used practical, herbal medical cures. The *ashipu* used magical ones. It seems that they were happy to work together, and the Sumerians had good reasons for using both. If, as they believed, the gods sent illness in a magical way then it made sense to use magic to cure the illness. On the other hand, herbal cures could be seen to work, and so it would be foolish not to use them, too.

Medical writings show that an *asu* had many herbal cures and could make anaesthetics (to ease pain) and antiseptics (to stop wounds getting infected) from various plants and minerals. An *asu* was trained to study the patient for symptoms and work out how to treat from that. The *ashipu* was also trained to look out for symptoms. These could be physical, such as stomach pains, or they could be things like dreaming of a dog, or even the color of a pig the *ashipu* passed on his way to the patient. The *ashipu* used spells and chanting on his patient.

◁ *This is the medical tablet discovered by archaeologists in Nippur that was translated by Kramer and Levey.*

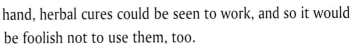

SKILLED WORK

One of the things that defines an ancient civilization is that the people divided up jobs and developed special craft skills. Instead of just making a cooking pot that does not leak or burst in the fire, specialist potters put a lot of time into the shape, smoothness, and decoration of the pot. Once this happened people began to trade the beautiful things they made for things they wanted, but could not grow or find in Sumer.

If we know about daily life mainly from the written evidence, we know about the skilled workers of Sumer mainly from the things they made. There are no tablets that tell a potter how to make a cooking pot, or a jeweler how to make a complicated necklace of gold. These workers were skilled with their hands, but could not read or write. They learned by working at their job from their youth, taught by older workers. They began by sweeping the workshop, fetching and carrying supplies, and running errands. As they gained more knowledge they moved on from the easiest jobs to more complicated work.

A single nail

Archaeologists think that beautifully made copper nails, like this one, were used in a ceremony when a temple was built, extended, or repaired. They were probably buried in the ground when the work was begun. Copper was expensive, because it had to be traded in from other places. So far they have only found nails like this while excavating temple sites.

Cylinder seals

Cylinder seals are very important artifacts. This is because they have early Sumerian writing on them. Most cylinder seals were made from stone, which is very hard to carve. They were tiny, about 1 to 1½ inches (3 to 4 centimeters) long, but full of detail. Because stone lasts well, archaeologists have found thousands of cylinder seals, all of them carefully carved with detailed pictures.

The people who made cylinder seals were skilled craft workers. They had to be able to carve beautifully, while keeping in their minds what the imprint they were carving would make on clay. Cylinder seals were rolled across a piece of clay, printing the picture on the seal in reverse. So the highest parts on the seal were lowest on the clay. The workers had to imagine the picture they wanted, then carve it "inside out" on the seal. Each cylinder seal was different. They were used as a mark of ownership, or as a kind of signature, on written agreements. People wore them around their neck, to keep them safe and to be able to use them at any time.

At first cylinder seals just had pictures on them. Later they had cuneiform writing, which tells archaeologists the name of the owner. Sometimes it also adds an occupation and the name of their personal god. From this we know that it was not just important people who used cylinder seals. It is not surprising that traders used them; it is more surprising that royal cooks and servants, even sometimes slaves, owned them.

△ This cylinder seal, belonging to Pu-abi, an important woman in the city of Ur, was made from lapis lazuli. Most seals were made from stone, but important people sometimes had several seals, some made from precious stones.

EYEWITNESS

"We are doing marvellously well. I'm sick to death of getting out gold head-dresses."

Part of a letter written by Sir Leonard Woolley to the archaeologist H. R. Hall about the 1928 to 1929 season at Ur, when he finished excavating the tomb of Pu-abi.

Jewelers

We know quite a lot about jewelry in Sumerian times, because jewelry was often buried with its owner. Also metal does not rot over time, like wood or even cloth. So we know that both men and women wore jewelry, and the most important people wore complicated jewelry made from gold and precious stones. Archaeologists have found tablets that tell us that temples and palaces often had their own jewelry workshops. Some necklaces were so heavy with precious metals and stones that they had to have a weight fixed on the back, to stop the weight of the necklace making the wearer lean forward all the time. The biggest Sumerian jewelry find was in the "royal graves" at Ur, excavated by Sir Leonard Woolley from 1927 to 1934.

Archaeology Challenge

Granulation

A small ring from one of the "royal graves" of Ur shows that Sumerian jewelers knew a way of working with gold called "granulation." This was where tiny balls of gold are made and then fixed to something else. In Sumerian times archaeologists have found that the fixing "glue" was a mixture made by boiling fish bones, a copper extract, and water. The whole thing was then heated to join together. It was not until the 1800s that Europeans found out how to do this.

◁ This statue of a ram caught in a bush was made with gold leaf, lapis lazuli, ivory, and precious stones. These all had to be traded in from other places.

Glass

Glass is very fragile, so not much Sumerian glass has survived. Glass-making workshops have been found, and the lumps of glass found in them show that glass was used mainly for small objects—beads for jewelry, tiny vases, and bottles. Blue was the most usual color, although it could be decorated with white and yellow.

Archaeology Challenge
Tools of the trade

Archaeologists have found a jar of equipment in a jewelers' workshop in Larsa (a city which was lived in, in Sumerian times and became important when the Sumerians were taken over by the Elamites). The tools help archaeologists to know how jewelers worked. The jar had tweezers, engraving tools, a stone for smoothing metal, and a small anvil and hammer, to beat gold into thin, flat sheets. The jar also held beads of agate, carnelian, hematite, and *lapis lazuli*. There were scraps of gold and silver, so archaeologists found out that jewelers saved these bits to melt down and reuse.

Casting with different metals

This bronze and silver bull shows the high level of skill of Sumerian metalworkers. Casting two different metals together, like this, needed a great deal of skill and knowledge. The metalworkers needed to know the different temperatures that each metal melted at, and they needed to be able to tell this without thermometers, as we have now, relying on the color and heat of the fire in the furnace and the state of the metal being heated.

TRAVEL
AND TRADE

Most Sumerians traveled very little. They stayed close to home, whether that was in their city or in the countryside around. City-states were not huge and produced almost everything they needed for themselves, so most people did not need to travel. Even kings did not travel far. The exceptions to this were traders, government officials, and soldiers when they had to go to war.

When they did travel, people walked or rode donkeys. They also used donkeys to carry heavy loads. Because they had invented the wheel, Sumerians could carry things in carts. Soldiers had war chariots to transport weapons and to fight from. However, Sumerian wheels were made of solid wood and so were very heavy. This made the carts and chariots heavy and hard to shift, even without anything loaded on them. Roads were just earth tracks, so the winter rains could flood them, or at least make them so muddy that carts stuck in them.

This silver model of a boat, found in a grave at Ur, shows a typical Sumerian boat shape. Sumerian boats were not made of metal, but of bundles of reeds tied together. It is very likely that the Sumerians then painted the outsides of the boats with bitumen, to make them more waterproof. This was what people living in the Mesopotamian marshes still did until the marshes were drained in 2002. Heavy cargoes were carried on bigger barges that were sometimes dragged along from the shore.

▷ These people are making a reed boat like the ones the Sumerians used.

Archaeology Challenge

Archaeologists know that the Sumerians had wheeled vehicles because they are mentioned in the tablets. However, the carts and chariots were made from wood and leather, which rots over time. Archaeologists have not found any actual carts or chariots, only a few pieces of wheel made of solid wood. The Standard of Ur shows chariots in more detail. You can see that the wheels were made of three pieces of solid wood held together with fixings across the middle.

One of the most useful and widely used ways of traveling was by boat, up the rivers and canals of Mesopotamia. Boats were especially useful for short journeys along canals. However, archaeologists think that people going north may have towed boats, especially heavy barges, up stream by walking on the river or canal bank. The earliest Sumerian boats were made from bundles of reeds tied together. The boats were paddled by one or more people depending on their size. Archaeologists have even found a model boat at Eridu that had a sail.

▷ Many smaller traders may have simply carried the things they had to trade on a wood or reed frame on their back.

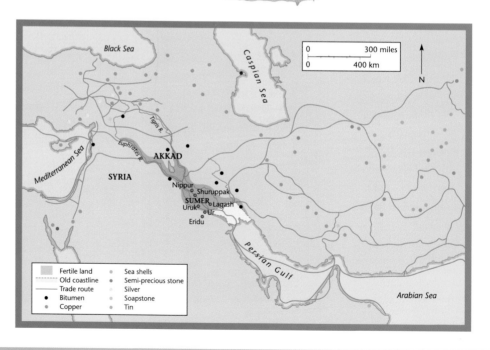

The Sumerians traded with peoples as far away as the Indus Valley, Arabia, and the eastern Mediterranean. This does not mean that Sumerian traders traveled all that way. It means archaeologists have found things made in Sumer in those places, and things from those places in Sumer. Most ancient peoples traded at a series of stopping points along sea and land routes used by almost all traders. The more stopping points there were before a trader bought something, the more expensive it was, because each trader had to make a profit on his step in the trade. Trading towns grew up along these routes. Many traders traveled in groups, because trade routes were a good target for robbers.

Archaeology Challenge

To work out where trade routes once ran, archaeologists have to use many different methods. Photographs taken from the air, or even satellite photos taken from space, can often show up well-traveled paths that cannot be seen from ground level. Written descriptions help, especially if several different groups of people write the same thing. Finally, the goods that were traded, where they have survived, also tell archaeologists how far the Sumerians traded, even if they do not show the stops along the way.

▷ *This map shows the most important Sumerian trade routes and the places they bought the goods their craft workers needed.*

Black Sea

Caspian Sea

0 — 300 miles
0 — 400 km

N

Tigris R.

Euphrates R.

AKKAD

Mediterranean Sea

SYRIA

Nippur
Shuruppak
SUMER Lagash
Uruk Ur
Eridu

Persian Gulf

Arabian Sea

Fertile land
Old coastline
Trade route
Bitumen
Copper

Sea shells
Semi-precious stone
Silver
Soapstone
Tin

What did the Sumerians want?

The Sumerians grew most of the food they needed. What they wanted were gold, silver, and precious stones—things they needed to make beautiful jewelry. They also wanted other metals, such as copper and tin, for their metalworkers to use. None of these things could be found in Sumer. The only thing they had plenty of that came out of the ground was the sticky bitumen that they used to make a waterproof coating on boats and buildings.

What did the Sumerians trade?

The Sumerians were lucky enough to grow more barley than they needed almost every year. So they could trade this with people who were not able to grow as much. As well as barley, they traded wool and woollen cloth, because this was something else they had plenty of, thanks to their many flocks of sheep.

Something different

This pottery jar was found in a Sumerian grave, but was made in Syria. The Sumerians made their own pottery, but this jar would have been seen as valuable because the decoration was different from the Sumerian style. In the same way, Sumerian pottery has been found in other places that made their own pottery.

ARCHAEOLOGY IN MODERN IRAQ

All archaeologists have to cope with the problems of conserving the artifacts and buildings that they uncover. As soon as something is uncovered, it begins to decay, affected by air, sunlight, heat, and damp. Archaeologists in modern Iraq have often had to cope with a more obviously destructive threat to archaeology—war.

The worst wartime damage has been in the 20th century, as weapons have become more and more destructive. During the First Gulf War the ziggurat at Ur was damaged and U.S. soldiers dug trenches through a site that had been found, but not yet excavated. One of the big problems is that soldiers want to be on high ground, for the best possible view. In Mesopotamia sites of ancient towns and cities are found on man-made high ground.

△ *This photo, taken in April 2003, shows the Deputy Director of the Baghdad Museum, Mushin Hasan, on his first visit to the Museum since the war and looting that followed.*

Archaeology Challenge

In the first weeks of the most recent war in Iraq, in March and April 2003, journalists were shown looted museums, especially the one in Baghdad, and told that there were many thousands of artifacts missing, destroyed, or stolen by looters who hoped to sell them. By June it was clear that the losses, although still great, were not this great. About 33 important artifacts were missing from the Museum and about 2,000 less important ones. Many of the "stolen" treasures had been locked in vaults under the major bank in the city for safekeeping before the war began.

WHO IS McGuire Gibson?

McGuire Gibson is Professor of Mesopotamian Archaeology at the Oriental Institute at the University of Chicago. Before the 2003 war in Iraq began, Gibson was consulted by people from the U.S. Defense Forces at the Pentagon about the importance of sites and artifacts and how best to protect them. Gibson showed them exactly where the Baghdad Museum was on a map of Baghdad, and left the meeting feeling sure that the U.S. Army would try to prevent looting. In fact, the U.S. Army did not try until it was too late.

Unlike the museum damage, the damage to archaeological sites has been greater than first thought. This is not just because of soldiers digging trenches to fight. As archaeologists from all over the world tried to do what they could to help, it became clear that a lot of damage to sites was the result of looting. In May 2003 McGuire Gibson from the Oriental Institute at the University of Chicago was part of a group that visited Iraq to try to assess the damage at historical sites and the losses at museums. Archaeologists from many countries are now in Iraq, working with Iraqi archaeologists to do what they can to prevent further damage.

EYEWITNESS

"From the helicopter we saw about **a**ooters, digging below us. We landed and the soldiers from the helicopter moved towards the men, firing over their heads. In every direction there was fresh digging, fresh disruption."

Part of description by McGuire Gibson of his visit to Iraq in May 2003.

This helmet is one of the artifacts that is missing from the Baghdad Museum. It is made from electrum, a mixture of gold and silver.

Several different civilizations controlled parts of ancient Mesopotamia at different times. We are going to look at the first of these people: the Sumerians.

About 3750 B.C.E.

Earliest known walled Sumerian city was Eridu. It had been lived in by earlier peoples.

3500–2350 B.C.E.

The most important Sumerian city-states were Kish, Uruk, Ur, and Nippur. Most of what we know about this time comes from stories about a hero-king called Gilgamesh of Uruk, or descriptions written later, which do not give clear dates.

Wars between the city-states weakened them enough for Elamites from the east to take over for several years. The Elamites were eventually thrown out by Lugalannemundu, ruler of Adab, who ruled all of Sumer. When he died the city-states split up and began to fight again.

2455 B.C.E.

From this time we have a clearer picture of Sumerian history. The city-state of Lagash became strong under king Eannatum. Scribes began to keep accurate records of the present and the past, as far as it could be remembered. Eannatum died in 2425 B.C.E., and Lagash began to lose power. City-states fought until Umma under king Lugalzaggisi took over in 2340 B.C.E. He was strong enough to unite Sumer for a while. He tried to take over land in Akkad, but lost. The king of Akkad, Sargon, took over Sumer.

2350–2150 B.C.E.

Sumer and Akkad ruled by Akkadian kings. Sargon the Great took over Sumer in 2350 B.C.E. and ruled both Sumer and Akkad in 2279 B.C.E. He ruled from a city called Agade that has yet to be discovered by archaeologists. His grandson, Naram Sin, took over but had to face revolts in Sumer and attacks from people from the north east of Mesopotamia, too. These people, the Gutians, took over Agade and Sumer for a short while, but never had complete control over all of it. Finally the kings of Ur, who had taken over the city-state in about 2100 B.C.E. and were Sumerians, managed to gain power and drive the Gutians out.

2150–2004 B.C.E.

The kings of Ur slowly took over more and more of Sumer, until they controlled all of Sumer and large parts of Akkad, too.

2004 B.C.E.

Elamites take over the lands of Sumer. At about this time, the Euphrates River, which had made Sumer powerful by changing course, changed course again. It moved away from Ur and the Sumerian cities that had set up along its old course. This, added to the almost constant fighting among Sumerian city-states and made Sumer weak enough to be taken over by Elamites from the east.

After the Elamites drove out the Sumerians they ruled for a short time, only to be driven out by the Isin people. From this time on ancient Mesopotamia was often ruled by several groups at once, controlling different parts. The following list shows the major ruling peoples (earliest dates are approximate).

1900 B.C.E. – 1595 B.C.E.

This period is called the First Dynasty of Babylon. The Babylonian kings slowly built up their power and enlarged their kingdom. The most powerful was Hammurabi, who ruled from 1792 to 1750 B.C.E. He set down a system of laws for the country that have survived for us to read today. After his death part of ancient Mesopotamia broke away from the Babylonian Kingdom. This area, called the Kingdom of Sealand, stayed independent until it finally joined the Kassite Kingdom in 1460 B.C.E.

1595 B.C.E. – 1157 B.C.E.

This period is called the Kassite Dynasty. The Kassite rulers tried to rule in the way that those before them had ruled, so that people found the new Dynasty easier to accept. Eventually, even the rulers of Sealand accepted their rule.

911 B.C.E. – 612 B.C.E.

The Assyrians, from the north, took Mesopotamia into their empire. They had controlled areas in Mesopotamia before, but this was when they had the greatest control.

612 B.C.E. – 539 B.C.E.

This was another period of Babylonian rule.

539 B.C.E. – 330 B.C.E.

The Persians controlled Mesopotamia. They were finally driven out by the Greeks in 330 B.C.E. However they had been slowly losing power in the area for many years before that.

1325–1354

Ibn Batt tah was an Arab traveler who visited Mesopotamia on his travels. He visited the ancient city of Nineveh (originally called Ninua), which had once been the capital of the Assyrian Empire. It was largely destroyed in 612 B.C.E. when the Babylonians drove the Assyrians out of the area.

1787–1821

Claudius James Rich was a diplomat, explorer, and archaeologist who had a special interest in old languages. He was the first person to survey and carefully excavate the remains of Babylon. When he published his memoirs in 1812, it sparked a lot of interest across Europe, especially his account of the Babylon excavations.

1835

Henry Creswicke Rawlinson starts copying inscriptions from the Behistan Rock. These inscriptions were in Old Persian, Babylonian, and Elamite.

1847

Rawlinson finishes his copying of the Behistan Rock inscriptions. He sends a native boy to copy the hardest to reach parts, using papier-mâché bricks to take prints of the writing.

1857–1924

Jacques de Morgan was an engineer, geologist, and archaeologist. While excavating the Persian city of Susa he found a large black stone slab with cuneiform writing on it. This was found to be the law code of the Babylonian ruler Hammurabi. The stone was probably carried off to Susa when the Persians took over the area (539 B.C.E.–330 B.C.E.).

1869

Jules Oppert, a French scholar of languages, gives the Sumerians a name. He even says they were mentioned in the Bible (most European and American scholars at the time saw Mesopotamia as part of the Christian Holy Land and related places back to what they saw as their equivalent in the Bible). He says that Sumer was referred to in the Bible as Shinar.

1877

Ernest de Sarzec finds a Sumerian city, with clay tablets written in cuneiform.

1912–1914

German archaeologists begin the first thorough excavation of Uruk.

1922–1934

Leonard Woolley, a British archaeologist, begins work excavating Ur. His excavations are paid for by the British Museum and the University of Pennsylvania, who expect to keep a share of the artifacts found. Woolley is the first archaeologist in Sumer to use careful excavation in layers and detailed record-keeping while excavating.

1926–1931

Max Mallowan, a British archaeologist, joins Leonard Woolley's team. While working at Ur he meets and marries the famous mystery writer, Agatha Christie, who writes a detective fiction book set in the area, *Murder in Mesopotamia*.

1934

New law passed to make it harder for people to take archaeological artifacts out of Iraq.

1946

Fuad Safar and Seton Lloyd find the city of Eridu.

1948

American groups, mostly university funded, begin to dig in Iraq. One of the first is the University of Chicago which continued work there until 2003 and the outbreak of the Iraq War.

1953

Martin Levey, a chemist and student of the history of medicine, and S. N. Kramer, a Sumerian scholar, translate a medical clay tablet from the city of Nippur.

1984

Juris Zarins studies satellite photographs of Mesopotamia to find out where the old coastline and river lines were.

1992

Satellite photographs help Juris Zarins and other archaeologists to find the city of Ubar.

2003

The war between Iraq, the United States, and UK leads to damage of Sumerian sites and the looting of Sumerian artifacts from Iraqi museums. Staff at the Pentagon ask archaeologist McGuire Gibson for help in knowing which sites to protect. He gives them lists of sites and points out the exact location of the Baghdad Museum, but they are not protected.

agate
banded type of rock used in ornaments and jewelry

anesthetic
something that stops you feeling pain

anthropology
study of human origins, societies, and cultures

antiseptic
something that cleans a wound

archaeologist
person who studies the past by examining and scientifically analyzing old objects and ruins

archer
person who shoots with a bow and arrow

artifact
object made by people, such as a a tool or ornament. Archaeologists often use the word "artifact" to describe an object they find that was made by people in past times.

besieged
surrounding a place with an army to force it to surrender

bitumen
tar-like material that comes out of the ground. It is sticky when it is dug out, but dries hard and is waterproof.

caned
hit with a cane as punishment

carnelian
dull red or pink semi-precious stone

charioteer
soldier who drives a chariot, a two-wheeled horse-drawn vehicle

city-state
city and all the land around it controlled by the ruler of the city

communal
shared or done by members of a community

cuneiform
name given to the kind of writing used by the Sumerians, where the writer makes wedge shaped marks in clay

cylinder
tube-like object

date
to date something an archaeologist has to work out what time period in the past it came from

excavation
carefully digging away the earth that covers an archaeological site

festival
celebration, usually held at the same time every year, often religious

forensic
forensic examiners look at all the evidence about whatever they are studying in great detail and make reports on what they have found

hearth
place where a fire is lit regularly

hematite
reddish-black stone

irrigation
supplying water to fields by changing the direction rivers flow and building extra ditches

kilt
skirt worn by men or women

lamentation
song or poem expressing sadness

lapis lazuli
bright blue rock used in jewelry

levee
bank built next to a river to prevent flooding

loot
to break into a place, steal from it, and wreck it

mace
long heavy weapon

mineral
natural substance that can be needed by animals and plants for good health. Some minerals can be used for jewelry.

officer
person holding a position of authority in the army

official
person holding a position of authority in a government organization

papier-mâché
this is made by soaking paper in water and then squeezing almost all the water out until there is a squidgy mass that can be shaped and dried out

pottery
things made from clay

prescription
written instructions from the doctor describing what medicines must be taken by the patient

reed
water plant with straight stems that can be dried and used to made roof coverings, baskets, and other things

religious
to do with the beliefs of a person, or group of people, to do with a god or many gods and goddesses

scribe
person who writes things down

seal
Sumerian seals were used to mark clay fastenings on things, to show who they belonged to

settlement
somewhere where a group of people build homes to live and work together

shrine
special place for religious worship

siege
a place is under siege if the people inside are trapped by enemies outside and cannot get out

society
people living in an ordered community with shared laws, customs, and organizations

spearman
soldier who uses a spear as his main weapon

standard
flag that shows the sign of a ruler

stratigraphy
digging down a historical site layer by layer, carefully recording what is found on each layer, and exactly where it is found

tablet
Sumerian tablets were clay discs or oblongs, flattened so that they could be written on and so used as we use paper to write on today

tax
money or items (such as crops) paid to the state by individuals from their earnings

tell
raised area of ground, often under a town. Tells happen when the people in a country build with mud brick. As the brick crumbles with time, homes are built again, often on top of the crumbled brick, so over hundreds of years, the whole town has moved up from the surrounding land.

thermoluminescence
a substance that gives off light when it is heated is said to be thermoluminescent

time frame
specific period of time

tomb
structure where someone is buried

trade route
road or sea crossing that traders always follow to go from their home to the place they are trading with

ziggurat
Sumerian temple, built as a series of steps, each level smaller than the one underneath it

FURTHER READING

Bertman, Stephen. *Handbook to Life in Mesopotamia*. Facts on File Inc., USA: 2003.

Dembar Greene, Jacqueline. *Slavery in Ancient Greece and Mesopotamia*. New York: Franklin Watts, 2000.

Schomp, Virginia. *Ancient Mesopotamia: The Sumerians, Babylonians, Assyrians*. New York: Franklin Watts, 2005.

Service, Pamela F. *Mesopotamia*. New York: Benchmark Books, 1998.

aerial and satellite photography 5, 20, 40
afterlife 26
Akkadians 6, 7, 8, 13
archaeology 7, 42–43
armies 16
armor and weapons 17, 26, 37

Babylonians 13, 44, 45
Baghdad Museum 42, 43, 45
banquets and feasts 28, 29
barley 21, 41
bathrooms 31, 32
battle tactics 17
Behistan Rock 8, 45
Bible Lands 6, 45
board games 27
boats 38, 39
building materials 5, 31
burials 26–27

canals 20, 39
carts 38, 39
cemeteries 26
chapels and shrines 23, 24, 38
chariots 16, 17, 38, 39
cities 5, 7, 14, 18-19
city-states 14–21, 23, 28, 38, 44
clay tablets 6, 7, 10, 11, 12, 19, 21, 25, 28, 32, 33
clothes 29, 30
copper 34, 41
craft workers 15, 19, 32, 34–37
cuneiform writing 6, 8, 9, 10, 35, 45

daily life 28–33
De Sarzec, Ernest 7, 45
dictionary tablets 6, 8, 9
doctors 32, 33
donkeys 16, 38

Enki 13, 22, 23
Eridu 14, 23, 24, 26, 39, 44, 45
Euphrates River 4, 5, 14, 20, 44

families 29
farming 4, 12, 20–21, 23
festivals 23

flooding 4, 13, 20, 22
food and drink 21, 25, 28, 32
forensic archaeology 30

Gibson, McGuire 43, 45
Gilgamesh 15, 44
glass 37
gods and goddesses 13, 14, 22–23, 24, 25, 33, 35
government officials 11, 15, 19, 38
granulation 36
Gulf War 42, 45

health and medicine 32, 33
helmets 17, 37, 43
herbal medicines 32, 33
homes 31–32

Iraq 4, 42–43
irrigation 20

jewelry 27, 28, 30, 34, 36, 37, 41

kings/rulers 14, 15, 16, 19, 23, 25, 28, 37

language 6, 8, 9, 12
Levey, Martin 33, 45

magic 33
marriages 29
Marsh Arabs 5
metalwork 37, 41

Nippur 19, 33

physical appearance 30
pottery 6, 19, 34, 41
priests and priestesses 10, 15, 19, 23, 25
proverbs and sayings 12, 16
Pu-abi 27, 30, 35

Rawlinson, Henry 8–9, 45
recipes 32
records 12, 25, 28, 44
religious ceremonies 25
roads 38

Sargon 15, 25, 44
schools 10, 11, 25
scribes 10, 11, 15, 25, 44
seals 12, 13, 22, 35
sieges 17
soil analysis 21
Standard of Ur 16, 17, 20, 39
stratigraphy 14
Sumerians 4, 5, 6, 7

taxes 15, 28, 41
tells 5, 7, 18
temples 7, 10, 18, 22, 23, 24–25, 34
thermoluminescence 19
Tigris River 4, 5, 14, 20
trade 35, 38, 39, 40–41
travel 38–39

Ur 18, 24, 25, 26, 32, 36, 38, 42, 44, 45
Uruk 14, 15, 18, 45

virtual reality images 24
votive statues 23, 24

war 16–17, 38, 44
wheels 38, 39
women 15, 29, 30
wool 28, 29, 30, 41
Woolley, Sir Leonard 26, 27, 36, 45
workers 15, 19, 28, 34–37
writing 6, 7, 8–13, 35

Zarins, Juris 5, 45
ziggurats 18, 22, 24, 42